A Wild Ride

When a man's ways are pleasing to the LORD,
he makes even his enemies live at peace with him.

PROVERBS 16:7

Most people love the bumper cars. They
push the pedal to the floor and bump into as
many people as time allows. This is a three-
minute ride. Real life doesn't lend itself to
this way of life. If we purposely knock heads
with people, we're always feeling at war.
Real life means thinking twice about
initiating pain, purposely deflecting
the hurts aimed in our direction, and
not engaging in retaliation. That is an
eternal heaven-bound ride.

Poor Little Rich Girl

Listen, my dear brothers:
Has not God chosen those who are poor in the eyes
of the world to be rich in faith and to inherit the
kingdom he promised those who love him?

JAMES 2:5

The tabloids are full of stories about the rich
and famous. Most of the time the stories tell
of people who are lost—people who are looking for something. When we read about their
lives, their mistakes, their endeavors, we
should thank the Lord that not only have we
found Him, but that we are poor in the eyes of
the world. Our mansion is not on earthly soil.
Our kingdom will not be lost. Our mistakes,
our endeavors, will be forgiven.

Actions

Outward Appearances

*"For in the same way you judge others,
you will be judged, and with the measure you use,
it will be measured to you."*

MATTHEW 7:2

The waiter was not happy about serving four
women. His face plainly read, "They'll leave
a little-or-nothing tip." He judged us by our
looks, not by our worth. In one way or another,
we're all guilty of doing this. The waiter didn't
know how to judge. We do not always know how
to judge. But You do, Father. You judge by our
hearts, not by our looks or our pocketbooks.

Actions

Life in the Fast Lane

He who trusts in himself is a fool,
but he who walks in wisdom is kept safe.

PROVERBS 28:26

Think of the three-lane freeway. The inside
lane has long been designated for speeders.
They eat danger for breakfast. The middle lane
is for Joe Average. He eats contemplation for
breakfast. The outside lane is for the cautious.
They eat responsibility for breakfast. Lord,
You watch over us no matter which lane we
travel, and You gently nudge us toward
that outside lane because You want
us safe.

Show Me the Money!

*Then they believed his promises
and sang his praise.*

PSALM 106:12

For almost every endeavor in life there are
rules that should be followed. Too often,
we want proof that there will be a reward
before we make a true effort. Lord, Your
promise is unfailing if we're only willing
to believe and wait.

Actions

A Bug's Life

*But avoid foolish controversies and genealogies
and arguments and quarrels about the law,
because these are unprofitable and useless.*

TITUS 3:9

The sign warns: GIANT ANT HILL—DON'T SIT
HERE. But it's the only clear spot on the grassy
knoll. It calls to picnickers. First one group
and then another spread out their blankets,
only to move within a few minutes. Ant bites
are no fun. If only we would feel such pricks of
foreboding when we ignore God's warnings:
Don't steal, don't lie, don't covet. . . . Just like
the picnickers, we sometimes pretend the
message isn't meant for us.

Clean at Last

" 'AND NOW WHAT ARE YOU WAITING FOR?
GET UP, BE BAPTIZED AND WASH YOUR SINS AWAY,
CALLING ON HIS NAME.' "
ACTS 22:16

After four days in the woods, our feet are dusty,
our hair is limp, and our faces feel like leather.
Camping is hard work. Ask any man and he'll
tell you the best thing about camping is the
riding, the exploring, the grilling, the quiet.
He's wrong. The best thing about camping is
the shower you take right when you get home.
Oh, how wonderful it feels to be clean! Lord, we
can have that kind of feeling with You when You
wash away our sins.

Window-shopping

*"Again, the kingdom of heaven is like
a merchant looking for fine pearls."*

MATTHEW 13:45

Three stores were out of the merchandise. The
first didn't carry it at all. *What kind of store is
this?* The second suggested a sister store. Hah!
Not a chance. The third suggested a major
chain store. Finally, tired and irritated, the
customer leaves without making a purchase.
Lord, You never fail to deliver or tell us to
go elsewhere. You are like one-stop
shopping. You provide everything
we need.

A Truly Great Man

For as in Adam all died,
so in Christ all will be made alive.

1 CORINTHIANS 15:22

Some funerals go on for hours, with eulogies
that tell of greatness. Some funerals go on for
minutes, with eulogies that focus around the
beatitudes. One funeral highlights works; the
other highlights the heart. Lord, I pray that my
funeral highlights a believer who is alive
with You.

15

Change

Not the Squeaky Wheel

He gives strength to the weary
and increases the power of the weak.

ISAIAH 40:29

Recently I listened to a fellow Christian, a
woman who is quiet by nature, as she talked
about her humbling experience helping others
in hurricane-ravaged New Orleans. Her eyes
were opened to the human experience, and
she is a better, stronger person because of her
deeds. Her heart was touched in a way that
suddenly made me realize she knows and feels
something I am still looking for. Open our
eyes, Lord. Lead us.

Change

Micromanaging

" 'If you do not oppress the alien, the fatherless or
the widow and do not shed innocent blood in this
place, and if you do not follow other gods to your
own harm, then I will let you live in this place, in
the land I gave your forefathers for ever and ever.' "

JEREMIAH 7: 6–7

Lord, sometimes when something displeases
me, I want it to change. I plan for ways to get
it to change. I offer suggestions to remedy
the situation and then sit back and hope
for change. Lord, usually it is I who need to
change. Help me, Lord, to be the branch that
bends. Help me to change.

Change

Rated G

> *"Choose for yourselves this day*
> *whom you will serve."*
>
> JOSHUA 24:15

The newspaper is spread out before us and opened to the movie listings. Have movies changed? Or have we changed? Most of the movies, we've never heard of. The others are ones we don't want to see. Change is an interesting concept. We either run toward it or we never see it coming. In this case, age has made us not only older but wiser. Some of these movies do not deserve an audience. Thank You, Father, for letting us grow into the knowledge that we need to feed our minds with what is good and pure.

Change

Fallen

"But blessed is the man who trusts in the LORD, whose confidence is in him. He will be like a tree planted by the water that sends out its roots by the stream. It does not fear when heat comes; its leaves are always green. It has no worries in a year of drought and never fails to bear fruit."

JEREMIAH 17:7–8

The tree looked sturdy and strong. Yet, torrential rains down a limb, and now the once proud oak appears flawed. When people pass the tree, they only see the broken branch and not the rest. What remains is still sturdy and strong. Lord, that downed branch is like the shedding of sin. Take it away so we no longer carry the burden. Help the world know us not for our weaknesses but for the strengths we owe to You.

Change

The Wisdom of Others

" 'This is what the LORD Almighty,
the God of Israel, says:
*Reform your ways and your actions,
and I will let you live in this place.*' "

JEREMIAH 7:3

Sometimes, Lord, the times when we think
we've done an outstanding job, we find out
that what we think and what others think are
not necessarily the same. And nine times out
of ten, the other people are justified in their
thinking. Lord, help us to do the best we can
and accept suggestions. We can grow only if
we're willing to bend.

Change

Days of Our Lives

"All men are like grass,
and all their glory is like the flowers of the field;
the grass withers and the flowers fall,
but the word of the Lord stands forever."

1 PETER 1:24–25

Look in the mirror. Can you still see the child who liked watching cartoons, the teen who liked bell-bottoms, the college student who liked makeup, the young woman who liked staying up late, the bride who liked to hold hands, the mother who liked to decorate à la Winnie the Pooh, the empty-nester who liked visiting her grandchildren? Lord, through all our ventures, You are the same and You guide us.

Change

A Willing Heart

"Consecrate yourselves, for tomorrow the LORD will do amazing things among you."

JOSHUA 3:5

They say that more people are led to Christ by friends than any other way. When I first started attending my new church, I didn't know a single person. I sat in the back and felt alone. I'd forgotten the first rule of friendship: To have a friend, you must be a friend. I made up my mind to get involved, to say hello to people I didn't know, and to make my presence known. It's working! My actions reinforced the knowledge that I was never really alone. I always had a friend beside me. His name is Jesus.

Change

No Editing Required

And the words of the LORD are flawless,
like silver refined in a furnace of clay,
purified seven times.

PSALM 12:6

The movie, adapted from a favorite book, failed to deliver. Oh, how I enjoyed every word of that best seller, but who was in charge of making this movie? The names were the same, as was the location, and occupations, but the plot—the plot had been completely re-done. Lord, people so often try to rewrite Your words. They all fail. The wonder of Your words is infinite.

Change

My Cup Overfloweth

*"I tell you the truth, unless you change
and become like little children,
you will never enter the kingdom of heaven."*

MATTHEW 18:3

Six months ago, the top rack of the dishwasher
overflowed with baby bottles and nipples.
Three months ago, half the space went to sippy
cups. Today there are a few cups and straws.
Lord, as I watch my son grow and change, I'm
reminded of how much You want us to grow
and change, ever stronger knowing You.

Commitment

Checks and Balances

"You have kept your promise to your servant David my father; with your mouth you have promised and with your hand you have fulfilled it—as it is today."

2 CHRONICLES 6:15

Oh, Father, how often good intentions open our mouths, and promises flow out without consideration of how much time we really have to give. Promises of the mouth are easy; they take a second to make. Keeping those promises is hard. Fulfilling them takes more than a second. We often fail to keep promises. I'm so grateful You set the example. You humble us with Your fulfilled promises. You make us want to be better people.

Commitment

Forever

My heart is steadfast,
O God, my heart is steadfast;
I will sing and make music.

PSALM 57:7

Glancing at my wedding ring I notice how
the diamonds have dulled over time. Some
might say, "Throw it out! Get a new one."
Others say, "Leave it alone. It's fine." I take
a toothbrush and some dishwashing liquid
and scrub. Soon the diamonds look like new.

Lord, thank You for my life. No matter
how tarnished I am, how tarnished
my life is, I can be cleansed and
You continue to love me.

Toiling On

Go to the ant, you sluggard;
consider its ways and be wise!

PROVERBS 6:6

"If you want something done, ask a busy
person to do it." Do you believe this saying?
Sometimes I do. Lord, let us busy ourselves
in Your ways. Let us constantly be adding one
more thing to do that will draw us closer to You.

Commitment

Just One More Thing

So then, those who suffer according to God's will should commit themselves to their faithful Creator and continue to do good.

1 PETER 4:19

I have an acquaintance who backs out of commitments at the slightest provocation. It amazes me to watch him blithely make other plans or even no plans at a time when he's expected somewhere. In some ways, though, he's saner than I am. He's not stressed, resentful, or overbooked. Lord, when the crowds pressed, when the disciples didn't listen, when You wanted sleep. . . Did You feel stressed? What a difference You made because You kept Your commitments. We can make a difference, too.

Commitment

And Two Shall Be Joined

"Let us rejoice and be glad and give him glory!
For the wedding of the Lamb has come,
and his bride has made herself ready."

REVELATION 19:7

Epiphany! Yet another biblical message
understood! Lord, when I open my heart to
You and welcome the Holy Spirit in, that's the
marriage proposal. I say, "Yes!" When I'm
immersed in baptism, that's the "I do!" Oh
Lord, You are a faithful groom—one who will
stand beside us forever if we let You.

Judgment

> *Nothing impure will ever enter it,*
> *nor will anyone who does what is shameful*
> *or deceitful, but only those whose names*
> *are written in the Lamb's book of life.*

REVELATION 21:27

Lord, a friend just dropped a bombshell at my feet. She shared a past sin that has my mouth hanging open in surprise. My first thought is *I don't understand.* My second thought is *Why should I understand?* My third and final thought is *Lord, help me to understand.* Oh Father, help us all to continually ask for Your help so that we understand and so that our name will be written in the Lamb's book of life.

Sight Unseen

*A faith and knowledge resting on the hope
of eternal life, which God, who does not lie,
promised before the beginning of time.*

TITUS 1:2

The wedding ring has no beginning and no
end. It is often used as an analogy, highlight-
ing the unending love between a bride and
groom. With a wedding ring, a spouse has
agreed to a promise of commitment, but too
often there is an end. With eternal life,
God promised before the beginning of
time. He gave us His Son to highlight
the unending love between a Father
and child. He has never strayed from
that promise.

Follow the Leader

"I am the light of the world.
Whoever follows me will never walk in darkness,
but will have the light of life."

JOHN 8:12

At the playground I watch two sisters: one big, one little. The big one jumps from object to object, never breaking a sweat. The little one cannot reach, but oh, she can stretch, and she so wants to follow her big sister's lead. She never gives up. Lord, I want to follow Your lead; and like the little sister, I sometimes feel I cannot reach. I will never give up, as I know You will never move too fast or too far for me. I'm committed to following You.

Commitment

Reading between the Lines

Keep reminding them of these things.
Warn them before God against quarreling
about words; it is of no value,
and only ruins those who listen.

2 TIMOTHY 2:14

Lord, across this nation there are churches
in peril because of debates over the interpre-
tation of Your Word. Oh, Father, how sorrow-
ful You must be over the lack of unity Your
followers display. Father, help us look to Your
Word. Help us to read Your Word and reach
true understanding. Help us to know You.

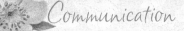
Communication

Raindrops Keep Falling
on My Head

"Take my yoke upon you and learn from me,
for I am gentle and humble in heart,
and you will find rest for your souls."

MATTHEW 11:29

The promised storm came at midnight.
Only instead of a bang as the weatherman
predicted, it arrived with a gentle whisper.
Rain pat, pat, patted against the roof over
my head. One-syllable words, over and over:

"I am here. I am here. I am with you."
Comforted, I return to sleep. There
will be a rainbow in the morning.

34

Ask and Ye Shall Receive

Until I come, devote yourself to the public reading of Scripture, to preaching and to teaching.

1 TIMOTHY 4:13

The yellow piece of paper tacked to the bulletin board at the store catches my eye. HELP FOR MOTHERS OF YOUNG CHILDREN. I taped the notice to my refrigerator. I often have questions; I always welcome help. The sturdy brown book on my coffee table catches my eye—Holy Bible. Inside is help available to everyone. I keep the Bible handy. It rests on the bedside table, it jumps to the coffee table, and sometimes it travels in my car. I often have questions; I always welcome help.

A Joyful Noise

Day after day they pour forth speech;
night after night they display knowledge.

PSALM 19:2

At almost any time of the day, children happily romp, climb, stumble, and scream in our mall's indoor playground. Sometimes a security officer calls for attention and asks that the children speak in their indoor voices. What he doesn't seem to realize is that the indoor voices of more than forty children combined equals one very loud, outdoor-type voice. Oh, Lord, wouldn't it be grand if the noise of Your followers proclaimed the message of Your Word as loudly and freely as these children proclaim their joy at playtime?

Dear Reader

*" 'You have made known to me the paths
of life; you will fill me with joy in your presence.' "*

ACTS 2:28

The letter came from an eighty-three-year-old
reader. She liked what I wrote, remarked on
my biography, and told me a bit about herself. I
always wonder what to do. Should I respond? Is
this person reaching out, needing contact? Or
is this person really just touching base and saying, "Yes, readers are out here"? Father, we are
readers of Your Word. We reach out. We need
contact. We thank You for providing us a means
of knowing Your presence. We are out here. We
are followers of Your Word.

He Knows My Name

> *"You have kept your promise
> to your servant David my father;
> with your mouth you have promised
> and with your hand you have
> fulfilled it—as it is today."*

1 KINGS 8:24

There are plaques that take John 3:16 and change the words, "For God so loved the world. . ." to "For God so loved [insert your name here]. . ." Just as God spoke to David, just as God knew David personally, so He knows each and every one of us, and keeps His promises to us.

The One to Listen To

Listen to his voice, and hold fast to him.
For the Lord is your life, and he will give you many
years in the land he swore to give to your fathers,
Abraham, Isaac and Jacob.

DEUTERONOMY 30:20

The telephone shrills, wrenching me from my
nap. A recorded voice begins some spiel about
mortgages. I hang up. I have no guilt about
hanging up on a computer. Father, throughout
the day we are bombarded with useless messages. But not from You. I say a
prayer before lying down for my nap.
I listen to Your voice and hold fast to
Your unwavering message. I hang on.

One Ringy Dingy, Two Ringy Dingy

"I am going to send you what my Father has promised; but stay in the city until you have been clothed with power from on high."

LUKE 24:49

Do you remember the anxiety of waiting for *the* phone call from the opposite sex? Girls hover near their phone and anguish with their friends about how to respond. Guys, on the other hand, seldom hover or angst. Weeks can pass before they think, *Hey, I should call her.* Seldom is a discussion among their peers needed to prepare for said phone call. Our Father promised to call for us, and we do not need to worry that He will fail to honor that promise. We do, however, need to prepare.

Put Your Hand in the Hand

We who are strong ought to bear with the
failings of the weak and not to please ourselves.

ROMANS 15:1

The Sunday school class is a tossed salad of
souls. My peers are young, old, learned, primer,
saved, lost, seeking. . . At different times, I've
fallen under the different categories. Just when
I think I'm strong, I realize I'm weak. When
I'm weak, You make me strong. And through it
all, I watch the struggling of my peers, as they,
like me, seek to travel the path of Your way. I'm
happiest when I'm not only holding the hand of
the person in front of me but also holding the
hand of the person behind me.

News to Me

> *"We tell you the good news:*
> *What God promised our fathers he has fulfilled*
> *for us, their children, by raising up Jesus."*
>
> ACTS 13:32–33

They say no news is good news. For the most part, I do not believe this is true. Now that I am a wife and mother, when the day grows dim and one of my loved ones is not where he should be, no news is scary and frustrating. Lord, You've kept nothing from us. You don't make us wait and worry. We know all Your news. And if we heed the message, nothing is scary or frustrating. We have Jesus to lead the way, to hold our hand. Thank You, Father, for the good news of Your promises and their endurance.

42

Community

Come to the Church in the Wildwood

For God, who said, "Let light shine out of darkness,"
made his light shine in our hearts to give us
the light of the knowledge of the glory
of God in the face of Christ.

2 Corinthians 4:6

On a recent trip, my husband and I pulled off the main road to explore a small town just six miles off the beaten path. We found Country Store Road. We traveled up one road and down another for about twenty minutes, and that was the entire town. There was no country store. But there was a church! In the middle of a town so small there wasn't a store. Lord, You truly are a light in the darkness.

Not Just a Number

We proclaim to you what we have seen and heard,
so that you also may have fellowship with us.
And our fellowship is with the Father
and with his Son, Jesus Christ.
We write this to make our joy complete.

1 JOHN 1:3–4

Years ago front porches were used for social-
izing. Today we don't always know our neighbors. Fences act as walls to keep the world at
bay. Lord, I've heard it takes a village to raise a
child. I also think it takes a community to nurture an adult. Thank You for Christian fellowship. Help us to grow stronger in the bosom of
Your church. Help us learn from the wisdom
of others who walk the path.

Knock and the Door Shall Be Answered

*"Here I am! I stand at the door and knock.
If anyone hears my voice and opens the door,
I will come in and eat with him, and he with me."*

REVELATION 3:20

Recently a friend shared a story about her mother's childhood. She said once there was a death in the family, and when the family came home from the burial, the house was filled with food. Neighbors had stopped by while the family was away. The mother's childhood, of course, was a good eighty years ago—back when doors didn't have to be locked. Lord, do not let locked doors hinder us from either sharing a meal or sharing Your promises.

The Résumé

We have different gifts,
according to the grace given us.

ROMANS 12:6

I keep looking for my place at church. Am I a
greeter? A teacher? A card writer? The Bible
says he who is last will be first. Our minister
quotes this often, yet I consider him to be more
important than I. He says that without the pew
packers, he'd be nothing. Oh, Lord, thank You
for the opportunity to lead, the opportunity to
follow, the opportunity to be involved in
Your will.

Wallflowers

" 'I tell you the truth, whatever you did for one of the least of these brothers of mine, you did for me.' "

MATTHEW 25:40

My husband takes the edger and tries to catch those stray strands of grass that grow too close to the cement. There are people at church who are like those strands of grass. They are the ones who stay on the fringe. Sometimes they are hard to reach. Maybe they long for acceptance, friendship, and fellowship. Lord, Your invitation includes everybody. We need to grab our Bibles and seek out the strays who grow too close to the world.

Creation

Plant It and It Will Grow

*But the word of God continued
to increase and spread.*

ACTS 12:24

Apple trees grow where apple trees probably shouldn't be. The owner of the cabin admits that for years she and her husband tossed cores in the dirt. Today, two apple trees provide a surprise delicacy for the area's birds. Sometimes, Lord, Your Word falls like those long-ago apple seeds fell—on the ears of people who are where they shouldn't be. Isn't it wonderful when Christianity spreads where Christianity wasn't before?

The Wise Man

"The LORD has kept the promise he made:
I have succeeded David my father and now I sit on
the throne of Israel, just as the LORD promised,
and I have built the temple for the
Name of the LORD, the God of Israel."

1 KINGS 8:20

What an undertaking building that temple was! Today on earth, building a temple is just as difficult an undertaking because we are the temple. The struggle to maintain, uplift, and nurture self—let alone a family—to follow the Lord's teaching is what every modern-day Solomon strives for. Lord, help us remember God's promise of redemption. Help us to build our temples on the rock.

Creation

A Rose by Any Other Name

*As for man, his days are like grass, he flourishes
like a flower of the field; the wind blows over it
and it is gone, and its place remembers it no more.
But from everlasting to everlasting the LORD's love
is with those who fear him, and his righteousness
with their children's children.*

PSALM 103: 15–17

A stranger handed my son a rose. In the backseat of my car, my eighteen-month-old played
with it for a few seconds, ate a petal, and then
tossed the flower on the floorboard, where it
eventually turned into a broken stem and
scattered pieces. Lord, when we try to
live without You, we are broken and
displaced just like the forlorn
rose. Thank You for the opportunity to grow in Your Word.

Scenic Wonders

"Your right hand,
O LORD, was majestic in power.
Your right hand,
O LORD, shattered the enemy."

EXODUS 15:6

The restaurant window provides a grand view of the ocean as the sun sets. I barely taste my food, so enthralled am I with God's creation. How can anyone doubt what the Lord has done? Has made? Perfection crashes against the beach as waves surrender to ebb and flow, and I am in awe of God's power.

Sunrise, Sunset

"See, I am doing a new thing! Now it springs up;
do you not perceive it? I am making a way in
the desert and streams in the wasteland."

ISAIAH 43:19

Sometimes the sun is orange as it sets in the west. It is breathtaking. The amazing thing about the orange sun is that the vibrant color comes from pollution. How can it be, Lord, that Your splendor overcomes such obstacles as the impurities in the air? How can it be, Lord, that You see past our imperfections and Your grace allows us to start anew? How can it be? It is the love of the Father.

Distant Lands

I'm a Traveling Man

"The LORD, the God of heaven, who brought me out of my father's household and my native land and who spoke to me and promised me an oath, saying, 'To your offspring I will give this land'—he will send his angel before you so that you can get a wife for my son from there."

GENESIS 24:7

Long ago, people seemed to stay in one place for generations. Siblings were a block away instead of a phone call away. Grandparents saw their grandchildren every day. Lord, what a blessing it is to know that we are all Your children, and that those of us who are scattered will someday be gathered as one.

I'm a Rambling Man

For the Lord watches over the way of the righteous,
but the way of the wicked will perish.

PSALM 1:6

Gates block off the living room from the rest of
the house. My little boy is sequestered where
he is safe. When Daddy and I are around, we
let him loose to explore the house under our
constant watch. Lord, we don't always stay
where we belong either. How glad our hearts
are to know that You keep constant watch.

Weary Travelers

*"The Lord is with you when you are with him.
If you seek him, he will be found by you,
but if you forsake him, he will forsake you."*

2 Chronicles 15:2

The television newscast spends much of its
time on the U.S. border issue. The illegal immigrants look haggard. The quest for a better life
is dangerous for them as it has been for Your
followers for so many years. I've never had
to travel the desert, to go without water,
clean clothes, and air-conditioning. I've
never known hardship. Lord, help me to
understand and try to make a difference, not only to those seeking a better
life but also to those seeking You.

God Will Take Care of Me

*Being fully persuaded that God had power
to do what he had promised.*

ROMANS 4:21

Missionaries often say how they know God
will take care of them as they spread His
Word in distant and sometimes dangerous
places. The most distant place I've been is
Mexico, to a church using car seats as pews
and a bathtub as a baptismal. There I saw the
look in the eye of a believer who truly knew
God would take care of him. It's a look
I strive for.

Doubt

Promise Keepers

By faith Abraham, even though he was past age—and Sarah herself was barren—was enabled to become a father because he considered him faithful who had made the promise.

HEBREWS 11:11

Abraham is a lesson about the mind-set of the doubters. No matter what God asked, Abraham did, and Abraham believed—believed for lengthy periods of time. We waste so much time doubting. Just think what we might accomplish if we accept God's promise and do what He says.

When in Doubt

He got up, rebuked the wind and said to the waves,
"Quiet! Be still!" Then the wind died down
and it was completely calm.

MARK 4:39

Sometimes, Lord, I feel hopeless. I am so
weak. I stumble. I cringe at the many sins I
commit. Then, Lord, You remind me of Your
disciples. Many were seasoned fishermen
and, at sea, even they were afraid of storms.
We are not worthy of Your grace, but our faith
will lead us toward victory.

My Prayers Are with You

*Even though I walk through the valley of the
shadow of death, I will fear no evil, for you are
with me; your rod and your staff, they comfort me.*

PSALM 23:4

The sympathy card sits on my desk. It has
been there for two weeks. I don't know what
words to write. My friend has lost a husband.
She talks of the void in her life and of feeling
so alone. I doubt my ability to comfort her.
You, Lord, know the words to write. They
are in the Bible. My friend is blessed.
She owns a Bible. She loves Your words.
They will do more good than the words
I am struggling to write.

Comfort Me

*Strengthen the feeble hands, steady the knees
that give way; say to those with fearful hearts,
"Be strong, do not fear; your God will come,
he will come with vengeance; with divine
retribution he will come to save you."*

ISAIAH 35:3–4

The babysitter opens her door, and my son
hesitates before going in. He checks to make
sure I follow. Inside, although the temptation
of other children beckons, he stays near my
leg, continuously patting my knee to assure
himself I haven't left him. Oh Lord, You open
doors, You invite us in, and we hesitate. Thank
You for the opportunity to follow and to study
at Your knee. You will never leave us. You are
always near.

Lest You Worry

*"Who of you by worrying
can add a single hour to his life?"*

MATTHEW 6:27

A friend of mine fears public speaking. Another friend will not drive on the highway. Me, I'm afraid of flying. These handicaps hinder our progress in life. They keep us from opportunities. Lord, You know our worries, and if we know You, we should be able to shed these worries.

Faithfulness

In My Father's Eyes

"For the eyes of the LORD range throughout the earth to strengthen those whose hearts are fully committed to him."

2 CHRONICLES 16:9

Recently, at a parenting class, I heard that if you really want your child to follow you, then walk backward. So, the next time we were at the park, and my son wasn't inclined to follow me, I walked backward. Guess what? He didn't follow. He still went his merry way. Lord, I wonder how many times You walked backward, keeping me in sight, and waiting for me to follow. Oh, Lord, I am so thankful that You never give up on me and that I am always within the viewing range of my Father's eyes.

Faithfulness

. . .As a Mustard Seed

*It was not through law that Abraham
and his offspring received the promise
that he would be heir of the world, but through
the righteousness that comes by faith.*

ROMANS 4:13

Sometimes we're guilty of thinking of God as a pseudo Santa Claus—one who has a list of who's been naughty and who's been nice. To make sure we're on the nice side, we want to have a whole list of deeds. But Abraham, one of the most honored and deserving fathers of all time, didn't receive the promise from God because of deeds. No, he received it because of his faith.

Where Are You?

But if from there you seek the Lord your God,
you will find him if you look for him with
all your heart and with all your soul.

DEUTERONOMY 4:29

One day the rearview mirror separated from the windshield of my car. For the first few moments, the loss didn't bother me. For the next few weeks—the time it took me to replace the mirror—every time I went to check my mirror I was bothered. You see, habit kept me looking for the mirror. As a driver, I was impaired. Lord, in so many ways You are like that mirror. You stand beside us, and sometimes we do not even realize You are there, but should we lose You, we are bothered, we are impaired. Lord, always keep us faithfully looking at You.

Volume Control

*And because of his words
many more became believers.*

JOHN 4:41

My husband likes the television volume set at 47. I want it at 17. We settle on 32, which means he can barely hear the words, and I am covering my ears. Lord, it makes me think of the Sunday morning sermons. Sometimes the lesson is over, and I realize I barely heard a word. Other times, the lesson is so powerful that, loud and clear, it seems to be directed right at me. Lord, we want to hear Your words. Keep us ever faithful. Never let us cover our ears.

The View from the Front Seat

For the LORD watches over the way of the righteous,
but the way of the wicked will perish.

PSALM 1:6

It's an indoor playground for children, and a
parent is supposed to be watching at all times.
I follow my son. I'm there if he falls. There's
another child lurching about, and I do mean
lurching. Soon, he climbs where he's not supposed to. His head is too close to the ceiling
fan, and I yell. He gives me a look and finally
climbs down. I am so grateful that my
Father watches over me, and He is
faithful. I am also grateful for the
watchful eye of the faithful who
do not want me to fall.

Delete

"Keep falsehood and lies far from me;
give me neither poverty nor riches,
but give me only my daily bread."

PROVERBS 30:8

My computer can connect me to other Christians. It helps me research Your Word. It also makes me vulnerable, because so much of the information about You is false. Help me, Lord, to keep my eyes open for only the truth.

Family

Father's Day

"I am the good shepherd;
I know my sheep and my sheep know me."

JOHN 10:14

The moon spills its light over the baseball
diamond, and the silhouettes of a father
and child can be seen traipsing across the
pitcher's mound. The father takes confident
strides. The toddler bebops about eight feet
behind. As if a magnet were holding him in
place, the toddler seldom strays from following his father's footsteps, and when he does
stray, the father stops, turns, and puts him
back on the right course. Jesus, You are like
that father. You lead, and I follow, and should
I stray, You want to guide me back on course.

Past, Present, Future

God sets the lonely in families.

PSALM 68:6

It's Friday and a holiday. I enter the hallway to my office and silence greets me. Most of my peers have taken the day off. In the quiet, I find the time to do the little things I've been putting off. Yet without the banter of my coworkers, there's the constant feeling that something is missing. Lord, part of the joy of the Christian walk is the fellowship of brethren, the feeling that all is right. We thank You, Lord, for the friends who lead us, the friends who walk beside us, the friends who are yet to come.

Unsurpassing

Children's children are a crown to the aged,
and parents are the pride of their children.

PROVERBS 17:6

If I could go back in time and change just one
thing, it would be this: my appreciation of my
parents. Too late I realized the precious gift
of their unwavering love. Too late I realized
the dedication they gave to guiding me in the
paths of righteousness. Too late I realized
that in the whole wide world, no one loves
like a caring parent. And, Father, I do
realize that You are the ultimate
caring parent.

Beloved

Give thanks in all circumstances,
for this is God's will for you in Christ Jesus.

1 THESSALONIANS 5:18

My parents didn't leave me; I left them—as adult children are supposed to do. While they were alive, I knew that should a need arise, a phone call would put them on a plane to come stand by my side. No one else has ever made me feel so perfectly loved. Father, please, somehow let the parents of unthinking children—those who don't say, "Thank you," or, "I love you," often enough—know they are indeed appreciated and loved.

Family

At a Brisk Pace

*"Success, success to you,
and success to those who help you,
for your God will help you."*

1 Chronicles 12:18

My aunt uses a walker. Lately, my toddler has taken a liking to the walker and wants to assist. He positions himself inside the walker, and she takes her position behind. Together they make a successful team. I have the same opportunity. I can position myself inside the Word and give You the position of leadership. Together, Lord, we are a successful team.

Beloved Mother

*"I tell you the truth, if anyone keeps
my word, he will never see death."*

JOHN 8:51

There are times that I miss my mother so
much that I reach out my hand and pretend
I can touch her. Oh, if I could only have the
chance to tell her again how much I love her,
tell her about my day, my worries, my joys.
Someone shared a prayer with me about
a ninety-six-year-old father. . .said they
couldn't imagine life without him. Every day I
miss my mother. Every day I'm one day closer
to seeing her again.

Someone to Watch Over Me

*"If anyone loves me, he will obey my teaching.
My Father will love him, and we will come to him
and make our home with him."*

JOHN 14:23

I wave good-bye to my husband as he goes off
for the weekend. I'll have two days just for me.
I can go to the mall and not be hurried. I can
go out to eat at the restaurant he doesn't like. I
can get together with my best friend. And yes,
those ventures are fun. But something feels
wrong. Lord, without my husband, there's
no one to come home to. Lord, if
You weren't in our lives, we'd always feel like this. Like there's
no one to go home to.

Secure Their Hearts

*"All this I have told you so that you
will not go astray."*

JOHN 16:1

Seventy-five percent of our young people
will leave the church when they leave home. I
think back to my own youth group. It is as if a
giant eraser had come down and rid the area
of those who once were my buddies. So I guess
that 75 percent is a realistic number. Lord,
be with our youth, be with their parents,
be with the church leaders. We pray that
100 percent of our youth will stay in the
church. We pray for the future.

Bless This House

"Honor your father and your mother,
so that you may live long in the land
the LORD your God is giving you."

EXODUS 20:12

A picture of my parents hangs above my desk. Both are smiling. They saw to it I was in church just about every time the door opened. They held my hand; they gave me shelter; they gave me love. They were about my age when the portrait was taken. Now they wait for me in glory. They were what God meant for a mother and father to be.

A Perfect Fit

And you also are among those who are
called to belong to Jesus Christ.

ROMANS 1:6

Legos are fascinating toys. They come in various sizes and shapes. Some Legos fit anywhere. Others have specific functions and only fit in certain areas. Try to put them in the wrong place and you wind up with either an awkward structure or one that tumbles. Lord, I want to be like that Lego that knows where it belongs. If I stumble down the wrong road, let me feel awkward so that I turn around before I fall.

Fear

Doctor's Orders

Jesus went throughout Galilee,
teaching in their synagogues, preaching the
good news of the kingdom, and healing every
disease and sickness among the people.

MATTHEW 4:23

A coworker goes under the knife this week.
He's a leader, a good man, a friend. The sickness caught him unawares, and now fear shad-
ows his every word and thought. We gather to
pray, give cards, and offer food. Lord, thank
You for caring for us, for knowing our
every need, and for giving us the
strength to face the unknown.

Fishers of Men

Search me, O God, and know my heart;
test me and know my anxious thoughts.
See if there is any offensive way in me,
and lead me in the way everlasting.

PSALM 139:23–24

They stopped by my office with a video camera
and asked for a fifteen-second bit defining
leadership. The first word that came to mind
was *courage*—courage to make a positive difference, not only in one's own life but
in the lives of others. Unfortunately, I
didn't speak my mind. I doubted my
ability. I was afraid I'd stutter, mis-
pronounce a word, embarrass myself.
They left. Oh how I want courage to do
right—to speak up and tell others Your way.
Help me, Lord, to have courage.

Snow Day

"Is this the one you say was born blind?
How is it that now he can see?"

JOHN 9:19

Snow fell. It coated the road and filled the terrain. Most drivers inched along at about twenty miles per hour. A few delusional drivers drove as if the roads were safe and visibility possible. Lord, how I talked to You during that drive when whiteness was the only color in my sight, when my hands were cemented to the steering wheel, and when fear gripped my heart. You were there.

Forgiveness

I'm Sorry

Then Peter came to Jesus and asked,
"Lord, how many times shall I forgive my brother
when he sins against me? Up to seven times?"
Jesus answered, "I tell you, not seven times,
but seventy-seven times."

MATTHEW 18:21–22

I missed a birthday. My grandmother's, no
less. I'd written a reminder on my calendar.
It's there. Why didn't I see it? Luckily, grand-
mothers willingly, with open hearts, forgive us
time after time. Lord, Your forgiveness, time
after time, is the biggest blessing of all.

Forgiveness

Hot to Cold

Have mercy on me, O God, according to
your unfailing love; according to your great com-
passion blot out my transgressions. Wash away
all my iniquity and cleanse me from my sin.

PSALM 51:1–2

I run my hand underneath the water and adjust the temperature. Right now it's running cool. I turn up the hot. Ah, just right. Then, I step in and yelp. Too hot! Lord, sometimes sin tempts us by appearing harmless, but like water temperature that can change in a moment's time, so can our involvement in sin. Water burns; sin does, too, but its scars run deeper. Guide our steps, oh Lord, and forgive and cleanse us from our sins.

Forgiveness

Calorie Count

*From the fullness of his grace we have all
received one blessing after another.*

JOHN 1:16

Why can't celery taste like brownies? I'd
never battle weight again if brownies had the
same calorie count as celery! Lord, sometimes the things we so desire are the things
that You warn us against. And, in the end,
should we partake, we experience the
repercussions. It will take me a good
year to shed the brownies that hug my
hips. I thank You that I can more
easily shed sin by Your grace.

Forgiveness

That Thing You Do

For the LORD GOD is a sun and shield;
the LORD bestows favor and honor;
no good thing does he withhold from
those whose walk is blameless.

PSALM 84:11

Lord, You position Yourself between us and sin. Oh, to be blameless. Oh, to always make the right choices. It's only through You that I can be blameless and forgiven. Lord, I recognize Your presence and ask Your forgiveness for all the times that I, like an errant child, didn't stay where I should.

Forgiveness

Step Free

The law was added so that the trespass might increase. But where sin increased, grace increased all the more.

ROMANS 5:20

I stand in a puddle in the middle of the parking lot. It's not a big puddle. One step in any direction and I'm on dry land. Sometimes as I sit in Bible classes and listen to the learned teachers talk about grace, I understand the concept. I am a child of God and often wind up where I don't belong—in a puddle—and grace surrounds me like dry land. I have only to step toward it and You.

Forgiveness

And Forget

The grace of our Lord was poured out on me
abundantly, along with the faith and love
that are in Christ Jesus.

1 TIMOTHY 1:14

I worry that if I'm not forgetting, I may not be
forgiving. Can you have one without having
the other? How many times can you profess
forgiveness for an offense committed over
and over? Oh Father, I am so grateful I am
not the judge—You are. We are so grateful that
You are the giver of grace. A grace we do
not deserve but You give anyway.

Friendship

At All Times

"Has his unfailing love vanished forever?
Has his promise failed for all time?"

PSALM 77:8

In the middle of the night, when all is quiet,
and the loneliness settles like a gray blanket
of fear, sometimes we question God. "Why
am I single?" "Why am I fat?" "Why am I in
a job I don't like?" "Why am I. . .?" "Why am
I. . .?" Maybe we should instead say,
"Blessed am I!" In the middle of the
night, when all is quiet, and the loneliness settles like a gray blanket of fear,
we can be comforted in knowing we
have a God to talk to.

You've Got a Friend

Whoever obeys his command will come to no harm,
and the wise heart will know the
proper time and procedure.

ECCLESIASTES 8:5

I'm meeting a friend for lunch today. She's
been a part of my life for two decades. Yet it's
been almost a year since I've seen her last.
How sad that life gets so busy that friends
are times and dates in my appointment book
rather than people in my daily walk. Father,
You are the friend who is constant. I don't
have to make time for You. You are time.

Friendship

Out with the Old

But Lot's wife looked back,
and she became a pillar of salt.

GENESIS 19:26

Now that I'm a Christian, I've felt distance
from my old life in the world. The life where
friends would call out of the blue to sug-
gest an R-rated movie, engage in gossip, or
perhaps even barhop. Sometimes, Lord, I
miss that life. When our lives change and we
struggle with the change, help us to let go of
the old life and faithfully run toward the new.

Friendship

Camaraderie

"In my Father's house are many rooms. . . .
I am going there to prepare a place for you."

JOHN 14:2

Why do I wait for the last minute to prepare?
I went to three stores looking for quiche.
Quiche? I wind up with bread. Will anyone
notice? Probably not. As the meal begins, food
takes a backseat to fellowship. Thank You, Lord,
for the gatherings of Christian women where
we lift each other up. Thank You for preparing a
place for me both on this earth and with
You in eternity.

Gifts

All That Glitters

And this is what he promised us—
even eternal life.

1 John 2:25

Another Father's Day has passed. Gifts are
spread out on the table: a tie, a travel bag,
a calculator, and by the door is a unicycle.
Were the gifts wanted? Needed? These gifts,
except for the unicycle, will take up space
in the bottom drawer. The unicycle will
be banned to the garage. We praise You,
oh Father, because You know what we
want; but more importantly, You know
what we need.

Gifts

Nature's Way

If any of you lacks wisdom, he should ask God,
who gives generously to all without finding fault,
and it will be given to him.

JAMES 1:5

As I sit at the picnic table and type, the hum of
hundreds of bees attracts my attention. After
a moment, the humming stops as the last bee
enters the opening in the tree. That's when
I really notice the storm clouds and distant
thundering. The bees knew the skies were
about to open up and unleash God-given rain.
I pack up my laptop and head inside. The same
God who gave wisdom to the bees also gave
wisdom to me. Thank You, Lord.

Beautiful Music

Sing joyfully to the LORD, you righteous;
it is fitting for the upright to praise him.

PSALM 33:1

My husband stands next to me at church. His lips do not move. I look around and notice there are others who do not sing. . . . How can this be? Singing is such a joyful activity, such a gift. My husband blames his voice. Another friend blames her shyness. I'm sure I've assaulted the ears of many of my pew mates with bad notes. But, Lord, can You hear me? My heart is filled with the wonder of You while I sing and listen to the words of praise.

Gifts

Celebrate

*Train a child in the way he should go,
and when he is old he will not turn from it.*

Proverbs 22:6

One by one the shower gifts circle the room.
Guests paw through bibs and colorful toys and
stroke velvet dresses and crocheted blankets.
Diapers, in four different sizes, are stacked
in the corner. The mother-to-be glows. We
are her church family, gathered together to
celebrate a new birth. We give gifts that will
contribute to the child's now and the
child's future. The best gift of all
is a family who is no stranger
to Your Word. Lord, keep this
family walking in Your ways—
now and in the future.

I Love to Tell the Story

*"As you go, preach this message:
'The kingdom of Heaven is near.' "*

MATTHEW 10:7

At a recent women's group, one of the leaders put together a type of speed-dating activity designed to help those new to the organization meet those who've been around for a while. Roughly twenty people visited my table. Twenty times I answered the same questions: name, how long I'd been a member, favorite gift. . . Favorite gift? By the tenth time I'd told the story behind my favorite gift, I no longer enjoyed telling the story. But Lord, may I never get tired of telling Your story and how You saved me.

Just What I Needed

Grace to all who love our Lord Jesus Christ
with an undying love.

EPHESIANS 6:24

Grace is such an overwhelming blessing that
most of us dance around our understanding
of it. We have a hard time understanding the
completeness of it, the purity of it, the overwhelming comfort it offers. But, oh Father,
this is a gift, a promise, like no other. It sets
us free.

Gifts

Spread the Word

*Blessed is the one who reads the words
of this prophecy, and blessed are those
who hear it and take to heart what is written in it,
because the time is near.*

REVELATION 1:3

Statistics fascinate me. Just this week I read
that 50 percent of the homes in America are
void of books. That's right. There are people
out there who do not know the joy of reading
a book. God, that includes Your book! I am
humbled by the gift You've given me. I can
pick up Your book, read Your words, and take
comfort in Your promises.

Good-bye

Never Alone

"And surely I am with you always,
to the very end of the age."

MATTHEW 28:20

It sounds a bit like an oxymoron. Can there really be a good good-bye? We say good-bye to friends, families, homes; and sometimes we are moving toward new friends, extended family, bigger homes, but usually we're leaving people and things we feel connected to. Jesus died and many considered His farewell to be forever. Yet it wasn't a final good-bye because He returned. For you and me.

Good-bye

Beauty Is in the Eye
of the Beholder

*"Now I am about to go the way of all the earth.
You know with all your heart and soul that
not one of all the good promises the LORD
your God gave you has failed. Every promise
has been fulfilled; not one has failed."*

JOSHUA 23:14

Oh, how I value my life. I see my husband, my
child, my home, and I feel so blessed. Then,
I worry. Do I value them more than You,
my Father? Do I really understand all that
You have given me and what's to come?
I, too, will go the way of the earth. Am
I ready? Or am I like Lot's wife, and I
think too much of this earth? Father, help
me recognize Your promises. Help me run
toward what's to come.

Good-bye

Never Forgotten

*"I will search for the lost and bring back the strays.
I will bind up the injured and strengthen the weak,
but the sleek and the strong I will destroy.
I will shepherd the flock with justice."*

EZEKIEL 34:16

The pebble hits the water and sinks. Ripples fade to the edge of the puddle. Soon the waning evidence of the rock's existence disappears altogether. Lord, sometimes when one of Your followers stops attending services, he or she resembles that rock. At first a few people notice and may even make a phone call or send a card, but soon evidence of that Christian's existence disappears altogether. Lord, help us to reach out to our struggling brothers and sisters. Don't let us ever forget.

Graciousness

Words from the Lips

"For if you forgive men when they sin against you,
your heavenly Father will also forgive you."

MATTHEW 6:14

Often when someone annoys us, we carry a
grudge. And even when that person repents, we
remember his or her travesty and want vindication. How blessed it would be if, as humans,
we truly knew how to forgive and forget as our
heavenly Father knows how to forgive and
forget.

Going, Going, Gone

> *Wash away all my iniquity*
> *and cleanse me from my sin.*
>
> PSALM 51:2

I sit at the picnic table at my friend's cabin. I'm
surrounded by ponderosa pines, shrubs, rocks,
the illusion of the wilderness. I can see only three
other cabins in the distance. But I can count
the electricity lines. One, two, three. . .eleven
in all. If this were a painting, the artist would
leave them out. Lord, sometimes I feel this way
about sin. I am created in Your image,
and You love me, but sin has marred
my beauty. Then I remember You
are the artist who made me, and
Your grace can wash away the
evidence of my sins.

Committed

I have sought your face with all my heart;
be gracious to me according to your promise.

PSALM 119:58

David was the man after God's own heart. How
I long to understand, to share, to obtain such
riches. I am humbled when I think of David's
relationship with his God. I, too, want to seek
God's face with all my heart. I want—long
for—God's graciousness.

Heaven

Utopia

" 'And I have promised to bring you up out of your
misery in Egypt into the land of the Canaanites,
Hittites, Amorites, Perizzites, Hivites and
Jebusites—a land flowing with milk and honey.' "

EXODUS 3:17

Lord, how amazing heaven must be. As much
as we try to be of the world and not in the
world, we are bombarded with foul language,
violence, addiction. We are a people who so
much want to change others. We want them
to be strong, faithful, kind, like Jesus. How I
look forward to the heaven You've prepared
for Your followers—a land without sin.

Heaven

Role Reversal

"It will be good for those servants whose master finds them watching when he comes. I tell you the truth, he will dress himself to serve, will have them recline at the table and will come and wait on them."

LUKE 12:37

Many times in life, I've switched places. Once I had a mentor; now I am a mentor. Once I was a student; now I am a teacher. I've always noted the blessings, having been a giver and a receiver. I am an unworthy receiver when it comes to God's rewards. I am also an inadequate giver. Yet, the promise was made to me. It's hard to imagine a reward greater than heaven.

Heaven

Battle Cry

*"All those gathered here will know that it is
not by sword or spear that the L*ord* saves;
for the battle is the L*ord*'s."*

1 Samuel 17:47

Lightning cracks and thunder roars. I look
toward the heavens. On the right, I see blue
skies. On the left, I see black clouds. As they
war with each other, the battle cry of two very
different weather patterns sounds. We are the
blue sky. Satan and sin are the black clouds.

The battle cry of thunder is You, Lord,
warning Satan away.

Choices

My comfort in my suffering is this:
Your promise preserves my life.

PSALM 119:50

The curfew is ten o'clock; the movie is rated R;

the neighbor's party always gets out of hand.

Temptation calls me, Lord, and even though

I know right from wrong, good from evil, and

how to say no instead of yes, I am tempted.

Yet, as much as my human nature leans

toward pushing the envelope, I am

always grateful afterward that I know

right from wrong, good from evil, and

did say no instead of yes.

Heaven

Mine for the Taking

*I rejoice in your promise like one
who finds great spoil.*

PSALM 119:162

Spoil isn't always a negative word. Sometimes
it's what the victor takes after a battle. It's
what at one time belonged to another and now
belongs to you. Lord, You created heaven.
I want heaven. Please direct me toward my
heritage, my great spoil.

Home

Moving Vans

Jesus replied, "If anyone loves me,
he will obey my teaching. My Father will love him,
and we will come to him
and make our home with him."

JOHN 14:23

The room is empty. I place my hand on the
wall to say good-bye. For more than a decade
this room housed my bed, my record player,
my clothes, my books, well. . . me. Moving is
never easy. It comes with worries: Will I make
friends? Will I be happy? Lord, someday I will
move to a better place—a place with no worries,
with no stuff, and where everyone is my friend.
I won't need to pack a single bag.

Curl Up Next to the Hearth

*For in the day of trouble he will keep me safe
in his dwelling; he will hide me in the shelter
of his tabernacle and set me high upon a rock.*

PSALM 27:5

The rain pours down from the heavens. Batting a tentative paw against the screen door, the cat finds unexpected freedom and runs out into the dampness. He makes it a few feet before cold and wind and wetness stop him in his tracks. This is not freedom! He races back inside, to the warmth of his master's home. Lord, if only we reacted to sin the way that cat reacted to rain! Help us to always turn our hearts in the direction of Your heavenly mansion.

Birds of a Feather

*Even the sparrow has found a home,
and the swallow a nest for herself, where she
may have her young—a place near your altar,
O LORD Almighty, my King and my God.*

PSALM 84:3

If I find a dead bird in the front yard, I know
that the cat is once again attempting to thank
me for feeding him, for giving him a home.
The dead bird in the backyard is a different story. This bird was taken down by a
storm. I found no wounds, no evidence
of foul play. The sparrow was perfect
except for its lack of breath. Lord, You
gave me breath, and You keep me safe
in times of storms. I am once again attempting to thank You for giving me a home.

Home

Final Destination

> *"In my Father's house are many rooms;*
> *if it were not so, I would have told you.*
> *I am going there to prepare a place for you."*

JOHN 14:2

I'm alphabetizing caption ideas when I suddenly notice that the word *heaven* is followed
by *home*. How perfect. Suddenly, I feel special, at peace. Lord, heaven is the home You've
prepared for me. How special. How I long for
that peace.

Home

Eyes Open Wide

*"For whoever wants to save his life will lose it,
but whoever loses his life for me
and for the gospel will save it."*

MARK 8:35

Lord, what is life without You? The options
the secular world offers are short-term and
empty. Heaven is long-term and glorious.
Lord, the best thing about heaven is You.

Who Would I Be?

You are my portion, O LORD;
I have promised to obey your words.

PSALM 119:57

I just watched the movie about Hurricane
Andrew. Devastation, Lord. In some cases,
everything destroyed. How interesting to note
the different ways people reacted to losing
personal belongings. Some fell to their knees,
convinced they were being punished, picked
on, unjustly singled out. Others, Lord, knew
that material things are temporary
and that they hadn't lost You. We
haven't lost You.

A Better Place

*But in keeping with his promise we are looking
forward to a new heaven and a new earth,
the home of righteousness.*

2 Peter 3:13

Wars. Threats. Recessions. Assassinations.
Every day the news bombards us with the
shortcomings of an imperfect world. Father,
every day we fall short. How grateful I am that
You've promised us a better place.

Home

I'll Huff and I'll Puff

Blessed is the man who perseveres under trial,
because when he has stood the test,
he will receive the crown of life that
God has promised to those who love him.

JAMES 1:12

The wildfires burned recently and with them came the destruction of several homes. One victim told reporters that he felt oddly liberated now that he was, in essence, homeless. He recognized what so many of us fail to see. We're only homeless if we think the walls that shelter us on earth make up the home we should cherish. God has made for us a home that cannot be destroyed.

Home

Home Sweet Home

*My eyes stay open through the watches of the night,
that I may meditate on your promises.*

PSALM 119:148

My car crests the top of a hill, and I look
down at the city. It is dark, and the lights
from businesses and homes shimmer. One of
the homes is mine. Inside are the ones I love.
As I travel the final few miles to my earthly
home, I am reminded of my heavenly home.
I'm reminded because You are here in the car
with me.

Love

Only a Mother

"As a mother comforts her child,
so will I comfort you."

ISAIAH 66:13

I miss my mother. She—more than anyone
else—knew how to calm my storms. When I was
little and thunder boomed, poor Dad wound up
sleeping in my little bed while I cuddled next to
my mother. When I was a college student, far
from home, Mom's was the voice on the other
end of the phone who calmly said, "No, the tor-
nado won't hit where you live." Just her
words were enough to give me courage. Lord, You're there for us also.
You give us strength when we're
feeling frightened and alone.

Love

Surf's Up

"What kind of man is this?
Even the winds and the waves obey him!"

MATTHEW 8:27

The waves continuously roll. They never end.
One crests, then another, unending. Lord, the
ocean sends its water rushing toward the beach
much like You send Your unending love and
forgiveness rushing toward Your followers.

The Master Comforter

Praise be to the God and Father of our Lord Jesus Christ, the Father of compassion and the God of all comfort, who comforts us in all our troubles, so that we can comfort those in any trouble with the comfort we ourselves have received from God.

2 CORINTHIANS 1:3–4

When my son was a baby, there was a two-week period during which he would wake up thirty minutes after I put him down. My trusty baby book advised either letting him cry or getting him a drink of water. I did neither. I'd go into his room and pick him up and just stand there and hold him. He'd go back to sleep—leaving me feeling needed and loved. Lord, sometimes at night when nothing is wrong, we feel Your presence wrapped around us. We feel so needed and loved.

Love

The Glow

"You are my lamp, O LORD;
the LORD turns my darkness into light."

2 SAMUEL 22:29

Sometimes, Lord, we see love as if it were a lightbulb. It is a definite entity—there to conquer the darkness, guide us, and brighten our lives. Yet, at times, it can either dim (disappoint) or blind (overpower) us. Lord, You are a light like no other. You lead the way to a better life, where we will be neither disappointed nor overpowered. Your love never dims.

The Cat's Meow

*"Everyone who calls on the name
of the Lord will be saved."*

ROMANS 10:13

The meows get louder, more frantic, as my
calico cat demands breakfast, hours before
breakfast is necessary. Ignoring the cries
is futile, as this cat has no volume control.
Blurry-eyed, I set the can of cat food on the
floor and watch my feline dig in. She truly was
hungry, and she truly set out to get my attention. And because I love her, I rolled
out of bed hours before it was necessary. Lord, I need only whisper
to get Your attention.

My Every Need

*Like newborn babies, crave pure spiritual milk,
so that by it you may grow up in your salvation.*

1 PETER 2:2

In the black of night, my baby cries. I lie in the darkness. Sometimes the cry tapers off after a minute and I congratulate myself for my patience. Other times it goes on. And I crawl from my bed and head for the kitchen and his drink of water. Lord, You hear my cries and know exactly what I need. You are my drink of water.

Love

The Best of Times

My purpose is that they may be encouraged in heart and united in love, so that they may have the full riches of complete understanding, in order that they may know the mystery of God, namely, Christ.

COLOSSIANS 2:2

Bottle in hand, I quietly enter the darkened room of my son. He starts to reach for the bottle and then changes his mind. He wants me first and the bottle second. I see the understanding, the love, the trust in his eyes. Oh Lord, let us understand You, love You, trust You with the innocence of a child who knows he's loved.

Love

Forever and Always

May your unfailing love come to me,
O LORD, your salvation according to your promise.

PSALM 119:41

Children don't get to choose their earthly
family, and too many children do not experience a happily-ever-after kind of life. We, as
children of God, can choose to have a heavenly
family, a heavenly home. Lord, we thank You
for being a Father who is constant and who
welcomes us to a happy-forever kind of life.

Love

When My Father Calls

The Lord is not slow in keeping his promise,
as some understand slowness.
He is patient with you,
not wanting anyone to perish,
but everyone to come to repentance.

2 PETER 3:9

At the playground, I heard a continual barrage
of, "Michael, don't. . . Come here, Michael. . . .
Michael, watch out. . . . Michael. . . Michael. . .
Michael. . ." I want to find this Michael and
turn him in the direction of his father. The
Lord is like that father, calling us,
and waiting until we finally turn
to listen to His promises.

Love

I Do

*Not one of all the LORD's good promises
to the house of Israel failed;
every one was fulfilled.*

JOSHUA 21:45

It wasn't the best time for a last-minute wedding. The church was decorated for vacation Bible school. The whole building had a race car atmosphere. The bride and groom were flanked by fake tires and empty oil containers. They didn't care. They were promising forever. Lord, You also promise forever to a people flanked by imperfections. Thank You, Father.

Memories

Never Too Many

And you will receive a rich welcome into the eternal kingdom of our Lord and Savior Jesus Christ.

2 PETER 1:11

The road near my friend's cabin used to be dirt. Back then only a few cabins called the area home. Then came the paved road. Civilization soon followed. Lord, the locals miss the old days when a walk at noon was never marred by a passing car. Yet the onslaught of newcomers brought electricity, convenience stores, and even the sound of children's laughter. It makes me think of how we welcome visitors. Sometimes we like our church home just the way it is. We fear change. Thank You for a heavenly home that is just the right size for all.

Memories

Right and Wrong

"If anyone chooses to do God's will,
he will find out whether my teaching comes
from God or whether I speak on my own."

JOHN 7:17

Years ago, I became interested in a boy at
church. About the same time, the elderly lady
next door started attending church with me.
Taking her meant not sitting with the singles'
group, not sitting by this young man. After a few
months, the relationship fizzled. Now, I know
where this young man is, and it's not at church.
I'm so grateful that I chose stewardship, even
when it wasn't convenient.

Lost and Found Opportunities

"In a surge of anger I hid my face from you for a moment, but with everlasting kindness I will have compassion on you," says the LORD your Redeemer.

ISAIAH 54:8

Lord, there was a time during my youth when I equated being a Christian with being a nerd. Today I regret that I was so weak I willingly and purposefully hid my light. I thank You, Father, for Your compassion. Today I wear the badge of Christian with pride. I know Your promise and want others to know it, as well. I hold my light in front of me. And with Your compassion and Your help, I hope more of my friends come to know You.

Memories

What the Empty Chair Said

"The twelve gates were twelve pearls, each gate made of a single pearl. The great street of the city was of pure gold, like transparent glass."

REVELATION 21:21

At a recent Thanksgiving meal, my nephew was missing. He works at a restaurant. When I was his age, I, too, worked at a restaurant. The difference? Thirty-odd years ago, restaurants closed so their employees could spend time with family. Today, more and more businesses are open. The almighty dollar is winning. Father, when I read Your book, there is no talk of money in heaven. Lord, I thank You for Your promise of a place where there will be no more tears, no more pain, no more hunger, no more sin. . .no more will the almighty dollar win.

Tears on My Pillow

*Christ died and returned to life so that he might
be the Lord of both the dead and the living.*

ROMANS 14:9

In the middle of the night, my twenty-year-
old cat, Priscilla, climbs on the bed and cries.
Her mournful tune wakes us up. My husband
wants to feed her, but I know she's not hungry.
Her yowling has gone on now for six months.
She misses her companion, Aquila, our cat
who died six months ago. The sorrow this little
cat feels is nothing compared to the sorrow we
should feel when remembering our Savior's
death. Yet there's the joy, too, in the knowledge that we'll see Him again!

Memories

Biographies

" 'Here I am—it is written about me in the scroll—
I have come to do your will, O God.' "

HEBREWS 10:7

The details of a child's birth may fade but are
still held close to a mother's heart. Many of
the accounts of Jesus were written decades
after His death. The details of our Lord's life
never fade and should be held as close to all
our hearts as they were to the hearts of the
men who penned the inspired accounts. He
died so that we may live.

Morning

The Maker of Days

" 'You have made known to me the paths of life;
you will fill me with joy in your presence.' "

ACTS 2:28

The morning calls me. I stand at the back
door and see the vibrant, green grass. I
imagine the fresh air and how it will feel
on my skin. I have a book to read, and the
refrigerator is stocked with sodas. Yet there
is laundry to do, dishes to load, and groceries
to purchase. Today I choose the responsible
path. Tomorrow I may not be so
dedicated. Lord, You are with me
whether I toil or whether I dally.

Morning

The Conversationalist

In the morning, O LORD, you hear my voice;
in the morning I lay my requests before you
and wait in expectation.

PSALM 5:3

Before 7:00, there's very little traffic. Before 7:00, there's the desirable parking place. Before 7:00, the house, the town, the workplace is quiet. What a perfect time to talk with You.

Night

No Need to Count Sheep

*"Praise be to the LORD, who has given rest
to his people Israel just as he promised.
Not one word has failed of all the good promises
he gave through his servant Moses."*

1 KINGS 8:56

There are times, Lord, when I climb into bed,
shut my eyes, and fall right to sleep. I wake up
the next morning refreshed. There are other
times, Lord, when the events of the day, the
week, the month, follow me to bed and I lay
there in turmoil. Lord, with You as my friend,
how can I worry about my enemies? You constantly watch over me.

Night

Twilight Hours

The LORD replied, "My Presence will go with you, and I will give you rest."
EXODUS 33:14

My husband leaves to work the graveyard shift. I watch television, read, sew, and roam the house. Funny. . .during my single years, I stayed up because I wanted to. Now, during my married years, I stay up because I'm trying to fill the empty space created by my husband's absence. But the empty space I feel when he is gone is nothing like the empty space I'd feel if I didn't have You. Thank You, Father, for being there when I watch television, read, sew, and roam the house.

In the Driver's Seat

*"But small is the gate and narrow the road
that leads to life, and only a few find it."*

MATTHEW 7:14

Headlights blink at me as I travel the midnight road. Who are these people out so late at night? Why aren't they at home? It's where I'd rather be. My headlights shine into the darkness, helping me see, guiding me. Lord, You are the ultimate light that I should follow. When I venture into the darkness, please guide me home.

Nurturing

Yours for the Asking

"Give, and it will be given to you. A good measure, pressed down, shaken together and running over, will be poured into your lap. For with the measure you use, it will be measured to you."

LUKE 6:38

The woman asks for a ride home. We're at a busy gas station, and she claims she's about to faint. She mentions new medication. Lord, she's a stranger asking for help. I offer to pay for a cab. But when she realizes I'm heading inside the gas station to call and then to give the fare to the clerk, she hurries off. Lord, I want to be a help to Your children. Give me the wisdom to help not hurt, to help not hinder, to do as Jesus would.

Nurturing

A Child's Eyes

*In everything set them an example by doing
what is good. In your teaching show integrity,
seriousness and soundness of speech
that cannot be condemned, so that those
who oppose you may be ashamed because they
have nothing bad to say about us.*

TITUS 2:7–8

I walk to the babysitter's door and knock. Next
to me, my one-year-old mimics me and also
knocks. A few minutes later, I sneeze and so
does he—even covering his mouth! Lord, every
day people see me, what I do and what I say. I
should be as careful with my example to them
as I am with my example to my toddler. Open
my eyes to the world that is around me and the
thirsty souls I meet every day.

Nurturing

Mirror Image

*It is a land the L*ORD *your God cares for;*
*the eyes of the L*ORD *your God are continually*
on it from the beginning of the year to its end.

DEUTERONOMY 11:12

The child seat in my backseat used to face the
rear. I couldn't see my son while driving, so I
purchased a special mirror that enabled me to
see his reflection—to make sure he was safe.
Then he hit the age and weight requirement for a
forward-facing child seat. I purchased a special
mirror that fits under my rearview mirror. It is
constantly trained on him. Lord, just like with
my son, if we look, You are there, keeping us in
Your sight at all times—to make sure we are safe.

He Paid a Debt He Did Not Owe

*For the LORD your God will bless you as he has
promised, and you will lend to many nations but
will borrow from none. You will rule over many
nations but none will rule over you.*

DEUTERONOMY 15:6

So often we hear stories of those who get
into such dire financial straits that they have
to call 1-800-GETMEOUTOFDEBTNOW.
There's a saying: Neither a borrower, nor a
lender be. But our Father tells us to give our
cloak if asked. That's because we have Him.
We are not poor but empowered by
the Word. We have so much to
give—and we need to recognize
that money is the least of what
we have to offer.

Nurturing

My Heavenly Father

*How great is the love the Father has lavished on us,
that we should be called children of God!
And that is what we are!*

1 JOHN 3:1

I am never alone. You, Lord, are always beside
me. You know my thoughts, my desires, my
fears, my gifts. Help me to remember Your
presence and to always listen to Your gentle
words of wisdom.

Nurturing

Turn the Pages

Your promises have been thoroughly tested,
and your servant loves them.

PSALM 119:140

Promises are made with words. You, Lord, are
the Word. When we study Your Word, we are
comforted and rejoice. When I read the story
of Jesus at the cross, I am at a loss to com-
prehend the pain He suffered. But I know He
suffered for me, so that I, a Gentile, could look
toward a heavenly home. Lord, thank You that
Your words are lined with promises for me.

Onward Christian Soldiers

The Sands of Time

"Now I am about to go the way of all the earth.
You know with all your heart and soul
that not one of all the good promises
the LORD your God gave you has failed.
Every promise has been fulfilled;
not one has failed."

JOSHUA 23:14

So often we drift. We go to church; we fall away. We read the Bible; the Bible gets dusty. We talk to God; we gossip to friends. No matter what battles we face, the best place and time to fight them is with God by our side, constantly leading us toward a better place.

Be Like the Ants

"I foretold the former things long ago,
my mouth announced them
and I made them known;
then suddenly I acted,
and they came to pass."

ISAIAH 48:3

Lord, how often do we overextend ourselves?
We try to be everything for everybody and
wind up disappointing others, as well as
ourselves and You. Lord, help us to be careful
what we promise. Help us to be dependable.
Let us accomplish our tasks to the
best of our abilities and demon-
strate a job well done.

If the Roots Are Deep. . .

*"He will be like a tree planted by the water
that sends out its roots by the stream.
It does not fear when heat comes; its leaves are
always green. It has no worries in a year
of drought and never fails to bear fruit."*

JEREMIAH 17:8

Recently, while working at an old cabin, my husband cut away the drain line and discovered why the sink was backed up. Inside the drain line was a solid, tangled mess of tree roots. You see, the roots of a nearby pine searched out the water source and surely found an oasis. Lord, I hope my roots are as dedicated to finding Your everlasting water as this pine was in tapping into the cabin's water.

Aye, Aye, Captain

Help us, O God our Savior,
for the glory of your name;
deliver us and forgive our sins
for your name's sake.

PSALM 79:9

The sign in front of the church building states that A CAPTAIN WITHOUT A COMPASS IS LOST. The implication is that man without God is lost. Lord, keep us from losing sight of the Promised Land. Keep us ever thirsting to know You and follow You. Keep us moving onward and never getting lost.

You Can Do It

*If only I may finish the race and complete the
task. . .of testifying to the gospel of God's grace.*
ACTS 20:24

My son tosses his sippy cup on top of his
playhouse and then promptly cries. When he
realizes no one is going to magically appear
to retrieve his drink, he picks up his little
race car and throws it at the sippy cup. A few
minutes later, his cup is secure in his grubby
little fist, and now his race car resides atop
his playhouse. But he has what he needs by
forfeiting what he doesn't need. Lord, let us do
the same when we follow You.

In the Path of Others

"Come, follow me," Jesus said,
"and I will make you fishers of men."

MATTHEW 4:19

The car in front of me slows, speeds up, slows again, this time to a crawl, and finally, after hesitating, turns. I return to the speed limit, just in time to stop for a red light I'd have missed had the previous driver known where he was going. How often do we stumble because we've followed someone who is lost?

Lord, help me to follow You.

God's Helping Hands

"And now, LORD God, keep forever the promise you have made concerning your servant and his house. Do as you promised."

2 SAMUEL 7:25

Sometimes we forget to let God be the source of strength in our lives. We think we must do it all ourselves. Father, no matter how much and how often King David stumbled, he kept his eye on You. Lord, remind us to never doubt the salvation You promised us. We march toward a better place.

Patience

Daddy's Girl

Yet he did not waver through unbelief regarding the promise of God, but was strengthened in his faith and gave glory to God.

ROMANS 4:20

As a child, just before 5:00 p.m., I often waited by the screen door for my dad to turn onto our street and into our driveway so that I could run to meet him. It was the highlight of my day. I never doubted his coming, and as the minute hand clicked closer to the time of his arrival, I got even more excited. He was seldom late, and when he was, I still waited by that screen door—because I wanted to. I want to wait for and run to the Lord's promised return with such joyous anticipation.

Place and Time

Teach me to do your will, for you are my God;
may your good Spirit lead me on level ground.

PSALM 143:10

A parking spot opens in the lane beside me. I start to ease my vehicle over, but another car zips into the space. Instead of being grateful that I didn't hit the other vehicle, I'm annoyed I didn't get the spot I wanted. Lord, I need to change the way I look at opportunity. If one avenue doesn't work, I should look for another one without wasting time and energy lamenting the lost opportunity. Lord, help us to see that our place in life is according to Your timing and Your will. You gently guide us.

Patience

Hand in Hand

You turned my wailing into dancing.
PSALM 30:11

I married late in life. For twenty years I watched as friends married, had children, led the life I thought I was supposed to lead. And I wondered what was wrong with me. Today I shudder to think what might have happened had I married during those twenty years, when I was still so weak in the faith, still so lost. Lord, we thank You for strong marriages and strong desires to do right.

What We Really Want

And there appeared before them Elijah and Moses,
who were talking with Jesus.

MARK 9:4

Moses and Elijah! Really! Appearing years
after their deaths and talking with Jesus?
Amazing. I used to feel sorry for Moses. To
think he led the people, walked for years,
and yet was denied the Promised Land here
on earth. But he truly spoke with and
walked with God. The Promised Land of
milk and honey pales in comparison to
heaven. Oh Father, what joy to know
that someday we will talk and walk
with Jesus!

Waiting for the Sequel

Let us hold unswervingly to the hope we profess,
for he who promised is faithful.

HEBREWS 10:23

Hope is an intriguing concept. It has helped many a lost sailor through the storm. Yet it has wasted the time of many an errant soul. People buy lottery tickets, hoping for a windfall. The other day I watched as two children played in a pretend movie theater. The screen was fake. No movie would show that day or any other day. Yet the children stared, mesmerized at the screen. They were waiting in vain. We, who are Christians, are not waiting in vain.

Patience

I Want It Now

They will say, "Where is this 'coming'
he promised? Ever since our fathers died,
everything goes on as it has since
the beginning of creation."

2 PETER 3:4

On some items of clothes there is a sizing tag
that reads, ONE SIZE FITS ALL. Many shoppers
believed the tag. Recently, a word has been
added to the tag. The word is *almost*. Now the
tag reads, ONE SIZE FITS ALMOST ALL. The previous tag made a false claim. God's words are not
false. They never change. They are eternal. He
promised He'd return for all who follow Him.

Peace

Open Your Ears

I will listen to what God the LORD will say;
he promises peace to his people, his saints—
but let them not return to folly.

PSALM 85:8

I was in my thirties before I fully understood
the parable of the prodigal son. Before that,
I wholeheartedly understood the older son's
quandary. Ironically, in life, I was the prodigal
son. Lord, I'm so thankful for the lessons of
learned teachers. As I grow in Your knowledge, I understand more the importance of keeping my feet firmly on
the path to redemption.

Storm Chaser

*He got up and rebuked the wind and the raging
waters; the storm subsided, and all was calm.*

LUKE 8:24

The storm struck while we were two hours
from home. For a good thirty minutes, rain
streamed down the windshield and thunder crackled. Then came sunshine. Once we
reached our house, we prepared for the storm
again. Sure enough, dark clouds hovered,
lightning flashed, thunder rumbled,
and all died away. The storm, once so
powerful, had no fight left. But in the
distance, there was a rainbow. Lord,
sometimes sin is like that storm. It can
surround us, endanger us, but if we run
toward You, it will lose its power.

Worry Woes

*And the peace of God, which transcends
all understanding, will guard your hearts
and your minds in Christ Jesus.*

PHILIPPIANS 4:7

Imagine never feeling anxious again! Some people are born worriers. I am one. I worry about being nice enough. I worry about whether people like me. I worry about doing a good job. There's nothing I do not worry about. My tendency to worry has not added one day to my life, has not solved a problem, has not made me a better person. Lord, help me to turn my worries over to You. Let me know the peace of God.

Peace

Who Will Stop the Rain?

*[Jesus] got up and rebuked the winds
and the waves, and it was completely calm.*

MATTHEW 8:26

Rain pours down and reminds me of the windshield wiper that needs to be replaced. Why do
I only remember during storms? Sometimes,
Lord, You're like that windshield wiper. I most
often turn to You when the storms of life surround me. And You calm the storms.

Peace

So You Want to Be a Writer?

> *Do not let your heart envy sinners,*
> *but always be zealous for the fear of the Lord.*
> *There is surely a future hope for you,*
> *and your hope will not be cut off.*

PROVERBS 23:17–18

Lord, years ago I felt the calling to be a writer and, like a wind-up doll, off I went in all the directions I thought I should go. I forgot to look to You to see what You wanted me to do with this passion. I wasted years trying to find my place. My place was always with You. The moment I accepted the calling You intended for me, the rest fell into place.

Plenty

Name Them One by One

Blessings crown the head of the righteous,
but violence overwhelms the mouth of the wicked.

PROVERBS 10:6

When I was younger, the thought of eating
out or going to a movie by myself seemed
undesirable. Why, people might look at me
and think I have no friends. Today, after the
demands of a family, a job, a life chock-full
of duties, the solitary meal at a fast-food
restaurant with a book propped in front
of me is a luxury—except while I sit
there enjoying peace, I'm missing the
blessings You've given me: family,
my job, my duties.

Just a Brownie Away

"To him who overcomes
and does my will to the end,
I will give authority over the nations."

REVELATION 2:26

One of the sins I fight is gluttony. I'm usually thinking about what to eat for lunch while I'm chewing on breakfast. Lord, there is a point when I know I'm full, yet if there's food on the plate, and especially if the food happens to be, say, chocolate, I eat well past the point of enjoyment. What is wrong with me? Lord, help me to change. Help me to know when enough is enough. Help me to put down the fork and clear off the table.

Plenty

Come to the Feast

Command those who are rich in this present world
not to be arrogant nor to put their hope in wealth,
which is so uncertain, but to put their hope in God,
who richly provides us with everything
for our enjoyment.

1 Timothy 6:17

Hmm, the frozen crabmeat in my freezer expired two years ago. Two years! Where did the time go? I knew the crabmeat was in there, but two years? Two years! Lord, I live in the land of plenty—so plentiful that I actually throw away food. Thank You, Lord, for providing for my needs. Help me to take better care of what You've given me. Help me to share the bounty.

Prayers

Father Knows Best

"God is not a man, that he should lie,
nor a son of man, that he should change his mind.
Does he speak and then not act?
Does he promise and not fulfill?"

NUMBERS 23:19

There's a country song called "Sometimes I Thank God for Unanswered Prayers." Its message is very powerful. What it is saying is that God knows what is best for us, and sometimes His answer to a prayer is no. Dear Lord, thank You for having the wisdom to know when to tell me no.

Loving the Unlovable

"You have not strengthened the weak or healed the sick or bound up the injured. You have not brought back the strays or searched for the lost. You have ruled them harshly and brutally."

EZEKIEL 34:4

In the workplace, one colleague can make all the difference, especially when they're missing. Today Broomhilda was absent. Work was a dream! No one stumbled in late, glared at me, asked off-topic questions, or annoyed her coworkers. Then, Father, back in my office, I look at my Daytimer where I've written, *Pray for employees.* More than anyone else, Broomhilda needs my prayers. I bow my head to pray for Broomhilda. I hope someone cares enough to pray for me.

His Needs vs. Mine

"Do not be like them, for your Father knows what you need before you ask him."

MATTHEW 6:8

There was a time when every spare moment that came my way gave me opportunity to pray. I was fervently praying for one thing. Now I miss those days—the days when I was in such constant communication with God because I had a need. It's amazing to me, Lord, that You hear our prayers whether we ask once or we ask continually. Sometimes we need to say certain prayers, make certain requests, over and over. But You hear us the first time.

Self-control

A Lie Is a Lie Is a Lie
Is a Lie Is. . .

*You need to persevere so that
when you have done the will of God,
you will receive what he has promised.*

HEBREWS 10:36

The dictionary defines *perseverance* as "a quest to complete an idea, purpose, or task despite obstacles." Father, help us to run toward the fruit of the Spirit. The ideas, purposes, tasks there seem so appealing, yet because we are human, we often get sidetracked by temptation. Help us to leave behind the ways of the Cretans.

Taking the Time

*"You diligently study the Scriptures because you
think that by them you possess eternal life."*

JOHN 5:39

Lord, sometimes as I hurry to delete the too
many e-mails that clutter by inbox, I acci-
dentally delete something important. In my
younger days, I was that way about the Bible.
In order to clutter my days with other duties, I'd hurry through Your Word. I missed
so many important lessons. Lessons I badly
needed. Thank You, Lord, for leading
me to understand the importance of
reading Your Word and not delet-
ing it from my life.

All That Glitters Is Not Gold

The devil took him to a very high mountain and
showed him all the kingdoms of the world
and their splendor. "All this I will give you,"
he said, "if you will bow down and worship me."
Jesus said to him, "Away from me, Satan!
For it is written: 'Worship the Lord your God,
and serve him only.'"

MATTHEW 4:8–10

There is a new mall in my hometown. The
stores are modern and shiny. Water fountains
and valets cater to a snappier crowd. A
few miles away stands the old mall. It is
suffering from the disease of comparison. Lord, Satan offers us a choice
that looks new and shiny. In truth, he
offers nothing but despair. Help me never
be fooled by temptation.

Think Twice

*When words are many, sin is not absent,
but he who holds his tongue is wise.*

PROVERBS 10:19

The weeping-willow branch used for switching retired to a corner, well before the children of the household reached the no-longer-switchable age. Years later, one of the daughters finally asked, "Why?" The mother replied, "One day, while I was using it, it connected with my leg, and I realized how much it hurt." Lord, we often hurt others. And others hurt us. Only our weapon is words. Help us guard our tongues because, Lord, when we use them to hurt others, we hurt ourselves even more.

Self-control

Seek and Ye Shall Find

*"Acknowledge the God of your father, and serve
him with wholehearted devotion and with a willing
mind. . . . If you seek him, he will be found by you."*

1 CHRONICLES 28:9

My hand digs through my purse. My car keys
simply have to be inside. Exasperated, I turn
my purse upside down and the clutter of a
female, mother, wife, employee falls onto the
table. Once I push aside receipts, wallet, pens,
etc., I find my keys. Lord, sometimes our lives
get so cluttered with the daily duties of busy
females, mothers, wives, employees that we
lose sight of You. Help us, Lord, to keep You
forever in our sight. We need You.

Caution

The way of the sluggard is blocked with thorns,
but the path of the upright is a highway.

PROVERBS 15:19

Morning traffic is at a standstill. The fast lane
is anything but. The shoulder looks inviting.
Would anyone notice, care, follow, or should
I venture off road? Sometimes, Lord, we stray
from the way of righteousness. Lord, You
notice. You care when we're doing wrong. The
only safe path, right path, is following You.

Self-control

Not the Whole Menu

*Dear friends, I urge you. . .to abstain from sinful
desires, which war against your soul. Live such
good lives among the pagans that, though they
accuse you of doing wrong, they may see your good
deeds and glorify God on the day he visits us.*

1 PETER 2:11–12

The coupon was good for an appetizer, meal,
and dessert. I managed to do the appetizer and
meal justice. Then came dessert. Dessert is
my favorite part of any meal. Yet could I
enjoy this dessert? Did I need this dessert? Sometimes, Lord, we do things just
because we can—not because we should.
Sometimes, Lord, we don't do the
obvious—the sensible. Lord, give us the
wisdom to think things through and do what
is best for our bodies and our souls.

It Can Be Erased

*"Forgive us our debts,
as we also have forgiven our debtors."*

MATTHEW 6:12

The traffic infractions vary. Near the front of the room are the speeders. Some were handed a ticket by a human hand; others were sent a photo ticket in the mail. The red-light runners are near the back. In attendance are also the school-zone challenged, the tailgaters, and a few right-of-way violators. We're all traffic offenders. The reward for attending eight hours of defensive driving class is lowered points and affordable car insurance. We're all sinners. The reward for living God's Word has to do with life eternal.

Time

Missing in Action

*"Therefore keep watch because you
do not know when the owner of the house will come
back—whether in the evening, or at midnight,
or when the rooster crows, or at dawn."*

MARK 13:35

The clock in my kitchen broke. I threw it away.
Now, at least ten times a day, I check the wall
where the clock should be. Each and every
time, I'm annoyed because it's gone. Lord, no
matter where I am and what I'm doing, You are
always where You're supposed to be. Watching
over me.

Time

Wash on Monday

*May the God of hope fill you with all joy and peace
as you trust in him, so that you may overflow with
hope by the power of the Holy Spirit.*

ROMANS 15:13

I turn on the dryer, convinced that the clothes
need yet another cycle. Fifty minutes later
the timer sounds, and I open the door. I'd
spent fifty minutes waiting in vain—nothing
was inside the dryer. The clothes are still in
the washer. Some people spin like that empty
dryer. Time passes and they move, but
nothing is really getting done. They
are spinning in vain. Lord, we
don't want to be empty vessels.
We want to be filled with the
goodness of Your ways.

Jesus, Take the Wheel

> *Here is a trustworthy saying:*
> *If anyone sets his heart on being an overseer,*
> *he desires a noble task.*

1 TIMOTHY 3:1

My parents owned a station wagon before minivans became vogue. My parents carpooled to school, the skating rink, and church events. Often, they filled in for other busy parents. You see, I was an only child. And each and every milestone was carefully watched by my parents. They were the epitome of "involved." Father, You treat me like an only child. You are there all the time and "involved."

Forever and Ever

" 'Here's the bridegroom!
Come out to meet him!' "

MATTHEW 25:6

My dad, a soldier in WWII, saw my mom, just sixteen, from a bus window. He exited at the next stop and followed her to the picture show. The rest is history. They were married for almost fifty years! Oh, Father, when did I first see You? Did I follow You immediately? Help us, Father, to create a history with You that makes fifty years seem like nothing.

When Time Stood Still

"In the time of my favor I heard you,
and in the day of salvation I helped you."
I tell you, now is the time of God's favor,
now is the day of salvation.

2 Corinthians 6:2

The grandfather clock stands in the corner of the room. As far as materialistic goods, it is my prized possession. The only maintenance it requires is a winding once a week. Yet, too often, its gears grind to a halt because of my neglect. Father, sometimes we fall short, even when we have the best of intentions, the strongest of desires. Please keep us from falling short in our pursuit of You.

Time

Growing in the Faith

Reflect on what I am saying,
for the Lord will give you insight into all this.

2 TIMOTHY 2:7

There was a time when I didn't understand the prodigal son. I fully sided with the older brother. When I finally understood the true message of the parable, my mouth opened in amazement. What? The Lord will take me back no matter how far I've strayed, no matter how much time I'm gone, no matter what I've done? Hallelujah! My Father loves me.

The Air That I Breath

*Therefore let everyone who is godly pray to you
while you may be found; surely when the mighty
waters rise, they will not reach him.*

PSALM 32:6

They say organization is the new diet. Oh how
we long to make the most out of our time. I'm
a list maker, and as long as I don't stray from
the 1. Pay Bills; 2. Take Shower; 3. Go to Post
Office; 4. . . . I get things done. But let one
item go unchecked, and suddenly the
list is forgotten. Lord, reading Your Word
is on my list. It's last because I like to
spend time with You before going to
bed. But I don't want You to just be a
checkmark on my list. I want You and Your
Word to be as commonplace as breathing.

Time

This Is the Day

"Give us today our daily bread."

MATTHEW 6:11

Yesterday's done, tomorrow is but a hope, today is unfolding before us. Father, let us appreciate the opportunities that come our way every day—opportunities to appreciate life, family, and You. Today is my day.

Trust

Rescue Me

Turn your ear to me, come quickly to my rescue;
be my rock of refuge, a strong fortress to save me.

PSALM 31:2

My son is barely a year old. He is fearless in the water. He has no idea he can drown. What he does know, what he senses with his trusting nature, is that I am right there and will pull him up should he flounder. Oh, were I so fearless. Were I so trusting of a Lord who does pull me up when I stumble. Like my son, I know You are there, and I do not thank You often enough for saving me.

My Door Is Always Open

"Here I am! I stand at the door and knock.
If anyone hears my voice and opens the door,
I will come in and eat with him, and he with me."

REVELATION 3:20

The wind ripples through the elegance of
the ponderosa pines. I hear the chirping of
birds soon marred by the distant roar of cars.
They drown out the wind and the birds except
for the distinct rapping of a woodpecker.
Lord, the world often gets in the way. If we're
steadfast in following You, we'll glory in the
knowledge that this world will pass
away, but You will never disappear.
Like the woodpecker, You'll
always be knocking at our door,
wanting to come in.

Open Arms

*"For the Son of Man came to seek
and to save what was lost."*

LUKE 19:10

A toddler gets ready to go down the waterslide
at our local pool. A mother stands at the top
to situate him. A father is at the bottom to
catch the child. Still, there's a middle sec-
tion neither of them can reach. Lord, so many
people in the world are at the middle sec-
tion of life. They've gotten off to a good
start—raised in the church. With open
arms, people are waiting for them to
come back to the church. Yet they're at
a place in life where it seems the Word,
the prayers, can't reach them. Father, lead
them safely home.

Understanding

So Help Me God

When God made his promise to Abraham,
since there was no one greater for him to swear by,
he swore by himself.

HEBREWS 6:13

How often have we heard the remark, "I swear on my mother's grave"? The expression has always given me pause because I never thought it literally made much sense. I understand swearing more when thinking of our court system today. I think of a witness literally putting his hand on the Bible and really thinking about what he's about to say, just like when I put my hand on the Bible, to open it, I should be really thinking about what is inside.

Why?

Your beauty should not come from outward adornment, such as braided hair and the wearing of gold jewelry and fine clothes.

1 PETER 3:3

Both Peter and Paul speak against the braiding of a woman's hair. They say not to do it, and I, in my limited knowledge, have to seek understanding about this stipulation. It seems that the women both Peter and Paul referred to were not simply braiding their hair, but braiding their hair with strands of gold in order to elevate their position among the other women. I understand the lesson now. Beauty comes from within.

Fine Old Robes

*Let the wise listen and add to their learning,
and let the discerning get guidance—for
understanding proverbs and parables,
the sayings and riddles of the wise.*

PROVERBS 1:5–6

The main street of town is closed off. Cars, long past their prime, line the road. My husband's eyes light up. A vintage car show! What better way to while away a Sunday afternoon than studying the make and model of old cars? My Bible is opened wide. The saints of yesteryear line the pages. My eyes light up. Bible stories! What better way to spend an afternoon than studying the lives of Your apostles.

Understanding

Open My Eyes

*"One thing I do know.
I was blind but now I see!"*

JOHN 9:25

The blind woman entered the hallway and
went to the left. It's an empty corridor.
"Where are you going?" I asked. Lord, my first
inclination was to take her hand and lead her,
but instead, knowing she wanted indepen-
dence, I gave directions. "Back up, turn
to the left, and walk about twenty feet.
There are two chairs to your left. After
them, you'll find the door you want."
Lord, I also find such consolation in
making discoveries on my own. I find
them when I spend time alone with Your
Word, awaiting Your direction.

Show Me the Way

And as for you, brothers,
never tire of doing what is right.

2 THESSALONIANS 3:13

I once heard the phrase, "Back row Christian, front row heart." I've mulled over the content ever since. Does it mean someone who does much but avoids recognition? Or does it mean someone who is thirsting for knowledge but is still young in the faith? Sometimes I'm happy considering the definition to be both. Lord, who am I? How do I find my true place in my walk with You?

Understanding

Lost and Found

*"The LORD will guide you always. . .and will
strengthen your frame. You will be. . .like
a spring whose waters never fail."*

ISAIAH 58:11

After glancing at the map for the fourth time,
I take a chance and rely on my gut feeling and
turn right. I'm in a part of town I didn't even
know existed. Sometimes, I feel the same way
about my Bible. Thank You, Lord, for providing
us a roadmap that will never grow old, never
dull, and which constantly gives us new areas
to explore and learn.

Understanding

Better Than a Blank Page

"I am the vine; you are the branches.
If a man remains in me and I in him, he will bear
much fruit; apart from me you can do nothing."

JOHN 15:5

Sometimes I'm frightened by the task of writing my innermost thoughts, my prayers, my life, on these pages. What if I've interpreted scripture wrong? What if I offend? What if readers shake their heads and say, "Boy, does she need a good talking to." Then I remember the times in my life when I didn't let You near my innermost thoughts, when I didn't pray, when my life had nothing worth sharing. Lord, help me grow in Your Word as I try to put into words my thoughts about You.

Understanding

The Search for Wisdom

*For the L*ORD *gives wisdom, and from his mouth come knowledge and understanding.*

PROVERBS 2:6

Some believe wisdom comes from schooling. Some believe wisdom comes from common sense. Some believe wisdom means understanding an object, event, or idea. Some believe you must be born with the wisdom gene. Some believe wisdom is somehow learned. Proverbs tells us the truth. Wisdom is from the Lord. When we are weak in faith, wisdom eludes us. When we are strong in faith, wisdom is within our grasp.

Understanding

Wonderful Words

*Let the word of Christ dwell in you richly
as you teach and admonish one another
with all wisdom.*

COLOSSIANS 3:16

I hold the book away from me. Where are the words? No, no way can this be my eyesight fading. I'm only forty-something. A visit to the eye doctor proves otherwise. A day later, the glasses go on and the words return. What a relief! I can read again! Lord, sometimes we are blind to Your words even when we can see. Thank You, Lord, for opening my eyes to Your Word.

Welcome

Come to Me

*Now Moses said to Hobab. . . ,
"We are setting out for the place about which
the LORD said, 'I will give it to you.' Come with us
and we will treat you well, for the LORD
has promised good things to Israel."*

NUMBERS 10:29

There is nothing equal to a church home that
feels safe, welcoming, constantly growing.
Some churches are cold; some are scary; some
are conservative; some are liberal; some. . .
Well, the list goes on. Finding a good church
home is just a tiny taste of what heaven must
be like. All feel safe; all feel welcome; all can
grow to be more like Him.

Welcome

Weighing What's Important

*For physical training is of some value,
but godliness has value for all things,
holding promise for both the present life
and the life to come.*

1 TIMOTHY 4:8

I make time to go to the gym. It's an interesting place. I always find myself trying to change
into my sweats in some corner area where all
the perfect-bodied people won't see me. It's
not my social arena; it's not my life. I make
time to go to church. It's a necessary place, a
haven. I often find myself standing
amid imperfect people who welcome me. It is my social arena;
it is my life.

A Good Neighbor

*Let us then approach the throne of grace
with confidence, so that we may receive mercy
and find grace to help us in our time of need.*

HEBREWS 4:16

The summer storm sent my neighbor's tree plummeting to the ground. We gathered in her front yard. Funny how it's only in time of distress that some neighbors appear. We've forgotten that time spent on front porches used to encourage. Or maybe that downed tree makes us feel like we're not imposing and that we're actually needed. Lord, we need You during both times of distress and joy, and You are there.

No RSVP Required

Remember that at that time you were separate from Christ, excluded from citizenship in Israel and foreigners to the covenants of the promise, without hope and without God in the world.

EPHESIANS 2:12

At one time, it was politically correct to use the term *melting pot* to denote the mixing of nationalities. Now we say "tossed salad." I'm not really sure what the difference is. I know only that at one time or another, we've all felt like outcasts. We've all looked through a window at a party we weren't invited to. We don't have to feel that way at all when it comes to God. We're all invited to the feast.

Work

A Constant Companion

From his dwelling place
he watches all who live on earth.

PSALM 33:14

My cat lies next to me as I type. Sometimes I forget to appreciate her sprawled body that obscures my notes. Her tail that knocks pens on the floor. Her paw that hits the space key, putting twenty-five pages where five pages should be. When she's not lying next to me, obscuring my notes, knocking my pens to the floor, or messing up my page count, I miss her and hunt her down. Lord, You also are beside me as I work—always. I never have to hunt You down.

Get It Done

Each one should test his own actions.
Then he can take pride in himself,
without comparing himself to somebody else,
for each one should carry his own load.

GALATIANS 6:4–5

Sometimes, Father, we put off what we don't want to do. We secretly hope that the task will go away or miraculously get done without us. Sometimes it's our own inadequacies that keep us from finishing because we're afraid we'll do a less-than-stellar job. Sometimes, Father, what we put off doing is what we most need to do—walk with You and do Your bidding.

Keep the Ink Flowing

For this is what the LORD says—he who created the heavens, he is God; he who fashioned and made the earth, he founded it; he did not create it to be empty, but formed it to be inhabited—he says: "I am the LORD, and there is no other."

ISAIAH 45:18

The drawer must have had a hundred pens in it! It's time to do a thorough cleaning. I sit down and take a clean piece of paper. Most pens no longer write. Oh, they look fine on the outside, but inside they're dry and useless. Lord, sometimes I meet groups of people who remind me of these pens. On the outside, they all look the same, but on the inside many are empty and only a few work. Please, Lord, never let my well run dry when it comes to serving You.

Harassed and Helpless

"The harvest is plentiful but the workers are few."
MATTHEW 9:37

My husband is the fix-it professional around
our house. He has the perfect tool for every
job. Me? I believe in the power of the shoe.
The shoe can hammer a nail, kill a bug, prop
up a table leg, etc. My husband's tools last
a long time and accomplish more. Me? I'm
always buying new shoes. Sometimes, Lord,
the cost of a shortcut is more than a new pair
of shoes. Help us to take the time to do the
work right.

Work

Don't Let Me Wait in Vain

*For if you possess these qualities in
increasing measure, they will keep you
from being ineffective and unproductive
in your knowledge of our Lord Jesus Christ.*

2 PETER 1:8

Open the door, shove the clothes in, and push
the ON button. Later, head back to the dryer.
The clothes are still wet. Maybe I wasn't firm
enough when I pushed that ON button. Sometimes I worry that I'm that way with You, Lord.
I get out of bed, get dressed, go to church, but
when I come home, I realize I missed something. My ON button needed a firmer push.
Father, I'm missing opportunities to know
You. Nudge me ONward.

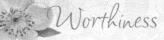

Worthiness

Who Is My Neighbor?

*He redeemed us in order that the blessing
given to Abraham might come to the Gentiles
through Christ Jesus, so that by faith
we might receive the promise of the Spirit.*

GALATIANS 3:14

Sometimes it's hard to realize that the "us"
He's talking about really is *us* and that we are
as worthy of His promises as Abraham. But
it's true. When I think, Lord, of the world that
surrounds me and the tossed salad of people I
encounter every day, I cannot even fathom
that You see us, all of us, as worthy.
But it's true. Lord, we are the Gentiles that Jesus gave His life for.
You love us, and we are important to You. It's true. It's true.

Worthiness

I Belong to Him

And the LORD has declared this day that you are his people, his treasured possession as he promised, and that you are to keep all his commands.

DEUTERONOMY 26:18

We so often look to our spouse, children, or friends, striving to feel accepted. Our Father already showers us with His love. How can we not acknowledge His promise? How can we not strive to keep His commands? We are treasured possessions!

Worthiness

Extra Clean Inside

"O Sovereign LORD, you are God!
Your words are trustworthy,
and you have promised these good
things to your servant."

2 SAMUEL 7:28

The used-car lot near my home has vehicles lined up, facing the street. Painted on their windshields are encouraging remarks: LIKE NEW! FANTASTIC DEAL! My favorite entreaty is: EXTRA CLEAN INSIDE. I'd like to think that, as a Christian, I am extra clean inside, but I know the boast is false, just like the boasts on the windshields are empty.

Still, God, You bless me with the Holy Spirit and with the promise of real things.

Splish, Splash

*He who has clean hands and a pure heart,
who does not lift up his soul to an idol or swear
by what is false. He will receive blessings from
the LORD and vindication from God his Savior.*

PSALM 24:4–5

Yesterday I paid a visit to the car wash. Today, as rain and mud splash against my hood, the pride I took in a clean vehicle subsides. But my car is clean and warm on the inside, and it provides me shelter. Lord, sometimes we forget to be thankful for what is most important: the warmth of Your Word, and the shelter of Your arms.

Worthiness

Ugly Ducklings

*"Why do you look at the speck of sawdust
in your brother's eye and pay no attention
to the plank in your own eye?"*

LUKE 6:41

It's often easier to notice the flaws in others
than to focus on their strengths. Why do we do
this? Does it make us feel superior? Maybe it's
because, like a red blob of paint ruining a fine
portrait, flaws tend to stand out. They're easy
to spot. Help us, Lord, to look past the stain
and focus on the beauty—not only our own, but
the beauty of others, as well.

Worthiness

May I Remind You?

*"O Lord. For the sake of Your servant
and according to your will,
you have done this great thing
and made known all these great promises."*

1 Chronicles 17:19

Father, I am guilty of redundancy. Should I
lay a request at Your feet, I feel the need to
remind You of my request over and over. I
tend to also remind You of my worth—though,
so often, I feel of no worth. I entreat others
to petition You with my requests. Lord, I do
this for me. You have been fulfilling promises
since the beginning of time, and I am blessed
to know You.

Scripture Index

Old Testament

To the minister who helped shape my childhood: LeRoy Davis
To the minister who helped me survive my maturity: Kenneth Hoover
To the minister who deals with the person I am now: Penney Nichols

Thank you, Lord, for learned men.

Cover design by Kirk DouPonce, DogEared Design

Published by Barbour Publishing, Inc., P.O. Box 719, Uhrichsville, Ohio 44683

Our mission is to publish and distribute inspirational products offering exceptional value and biblical encouragement to the masses.

 Member of the
Evangelical Christian
Publishers Association

Printed in India.

EVERYDAY

Promises

Spiritual Refreshment for Women

PAMELA KAYE TRACY

BARBOUR
PUBLISHING

Contents

Introduction

In the morning,
O LORD, you hear my voice;
in the morning I lay my requests before you
and wait in expectation.

PSALM 5:3

The Bible is full of answers, promises, and loving guidance. The best news of all is that we are offered the words of hope, the outstretched hand offering comfort, and the promise of God's unfailing word. We even have prayers to connect with the One who makes the promises. Hallelujah!

Actions

I Will Follow You

Direct my footsteps according to your word;
let no sin rule over me.

<small>PSALM 119:133</small>

My son exits the pool and walks across the
cement. He leaves little footprints as he goes.
Even as I follow him, they fade. Lord, You
left big footprints. Yet because of the Bible,
because of learned teachers, and because of
an intense desire to follow You, we can still
see Your footsteps, and instead of fading, they
become bolder.